QUICKREADS

LEVEL B • BOOK 3

Elfrieda H. Hiebert, Ph.D.

Glenview, Illinois

Boston, Massachusetts

Chandler, Arizona

Upper Saddle River, New Jersey

ALWAYS LEARNING

PEARSON

Program Reviewers and Consultants

Dr. Barbara A. Baird
Director of Federal Programs/Richardson ISD
Richardson, TX

Dr. Kate Kinsella
Dept. of Secondary Education and Step to College Program
San Francisco State University
San Francisco, CA

Pat Sears
Early Childhood Coordinator/Virginia Beach Public Schools
Virginia Beach, VA

Dr. Judith B. Smith
Supervisor of ESOL and World and Classical Languages/Baltimore City Public Schools
Baltimore, MD

Acknowledgments appear on page 9, which constitutes an extension of this copyright page.

ISBN-13: 978-1-4284-3151-5
ISBN-10:   1-4284-3151-9
9 10 11 12 13 V0UD 19 18 17 16 15

CONTENTS

CONTENTS

CONTENTS

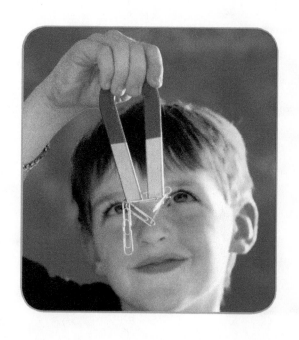

SCIENCE **Forces Around Us**

CONTENTS

SCIENCE **Thinking Like a Scientist**

Acknowledgments

Photographs

Every effort has been made to secure permission and provide appropriate credit for photographic material. The publisher deeply regrets any omission and pledges to correct errors called to its attention in subsequent editions.

Unless otherwise acknowledged, all photographs are the property of Pearson Education, Inc.

Photo locators denoted as follows: Top (T), Center (C), Bottom (B), Left (L), Right (R), Background (Bkgd)

Cover: Photos to Go/Photolibrary; **3** Photos to Go/Photolibrary; **4** ©IndexStock/SuperStock; **5** ©RCPPHOTO/Shutterstock; **6** Erin Hogan/Getty Images; **7** ©OJO Images/SuperStock; **8** ©Tetra Images/ Alamy; **10** ©Orange Line Media/Shutterstock; **12** Jupiterimages/ Thinkstock; **14** Jupiterimages/Thinkstock; **16** Photos to Go/Photolibrary; **18** Rebecca Emery/Getty Images; **24** ©studioworx/Shutterstock; **26** Comstock/Thinkstock; **28** Thinkstock; **30** ©IndexStock/SuperStock; **32** Best images/Shutterstock; **38** ©RCPPHOTO/Shutterstock; **40** Polka Dot Images/Thinkstock; **42** ©Suchan/Shutterstock; **44** North Wind Picture Archives; **46** ©Igor Kovalchuk/Shutterstock; **52** Jupiterimages/Thinkstock; **54** Erin Hogan/Getty Images; **56** ©MilanB/Shutterstock; **58** BananaStock/Thinkstock; **60** Stockbyte/ Thinkstock; **66** ©Purestock/Alamy; **68** ©Zurijeta/Shutterstock; **70** Jupiterimages/Thinkstock; **72** ©OJO Images/SuperStock; **80** ©Tetra Images/Alamy; **82** Getty Images; **84** ©David Young-Wolff/ Alamy Images; **86** Glowimages/Getty Images; **88** ©s70/ZUMA Press/ NewsCom.

Children's Games

Some games children play today are like games children played long ago.

Games of Then and Now

Today, children play many kinds of games with their friends. They use toys or balls to play some games. They[25] hide and find each other in other games. Long ago, children played with toys and balls, too. They also played games of hide-and-seek.[50]

Long ago, children had different names and rules for some games that children play today. However, many games that children play today are the same[75] games that children played long ago.

Today, children play some games on computers. Even tic-tac-toe, which children now play on computers, was played[100] by children long ago. They just played it on sand or dirt.[112]

Children's Games

Today, rubber balls are used by children to play games.

Games with Balls

Balls come in many sizes, but most are round. You can play many different games with balls. You can throw and kick[25] a ball. You can hit a ball with a stick. You can run with a ball. You can jump with a ball and throw it[50] through a hoop.

Children have always played games with balls. However, the balls used today are different from the balls that were used in games[75] of long ago. Long ago, balls were made of animal skins, wood, or even clay. Those balls did not bounce. Today, most balls are made[100] of rubber. With rubber balls, children can play games where the ball bounces.[113]

Children's Games

Long ago, children rolled hoops taken from wooden barrels.

Games with Toys

Over the years, children have played with toys like blocks, dolls, and stuffed animals. Today, children play with the same kinds of [25] toys. However, today's toys look a little different from the toys of long ago.

Long ago, most toys were made at home. Dolls might be [50] made of old socks. Round hoops for rolling on the ground might be taken from old wooden barrels.

Today, children's toys usually come from stores. [75] Many toys are made of plastic, not old socks or barrels. Plastic can be used to make almost any toy. Many toys use batteries. With [100] batteries, toy trucks can move by themselves. With batteries, dolls can talk. [112]

Children's Games

Hopscotch is a game that has been played by children for many years.

Games of Running and Hopping

For hundreds of years, children have played games in which they run and hop. In tag, the person who is[25] "it" runs after people and tries to tag them. In many games, people run with a ball. Sometimes people just run to see who is[50] the fastest runner.

In hopscotch, children take turns hopping through ten squares. On every turn, a player throws a stone called a marker into one[75] of the squares. To stay in a game of hopscotch, players have to throw their marker in the right square and hop over squares with[100] markers. Running and hopping games have been played in many ways for many years.[114]

Children's Games

Children often play word games by saying words and clapping their hands.

Games with Words

Word games can be played anywhere. Word games do not need any toys or balls. To play a word game, all you[25] need are some friends and words.

Some word games like "I Spy" are guessing games. In "I Spy," one person picks something in the room,[50] like a red lamp. The person then gives the other players a clue by saying, "I spy with my little eye something that is red."[75] The other players take turns guessing what the person sees.

In another word game, children clap as they say the words. The clapping games use[100] poems. Games like these have been played by children for many years, too.[113]

Write words that will help you remember what you learned.

Games of Then and Now

_____

_____

_____

_____

Games with Balls

_____

_____

_____

_____

Games with Toys

_____

_____

_____

_____

Games of Running and Hopping

_____

_____

_____

_____

Games with Words

_____

_____

_____

_____

Games of Then and Now

1. Another good name for "Games of Then and Now" is _____

   Ⓐ "Long-Ago Games."

   Ⓑ "The Games Children Play."

   Ⓒ "Games of Today."

   Ⓓ "Rules for Games."

2. How are games of today different from games children played long ago?

_____

_____

_____

Games with Balls

1. "Games with Balls" is MAINLY about _____

   Ⓐ balls that can be hit with a stick.

   Ⓑ games that do not use balls.

   Ⓒ different balls and games to play with a ball.

   Ⓓ how to make balls for games.

2. How are balls today different from balls of long ago?

_____

_____

_____

Review Children's Games

Games with Toys

1. How are toys today different from toys of long ago?
   - Ⓐ Toys today may come from stores and be made of plastic.
   - Ⓑ Toys today are made of wooden barrels and old socks.
   - Ⓒ Toys today are made only for young children.
   - Ⓓ Toys today are dolls and stuffed animals.

2. Retell two facts you learned in "Games with Toys."

_____

_____

_____

Games of Running and Hopping

1. The main idea of "Games of Running and Hopping" is _____
   - Ⓐ how to make a new running and hopping game.
   - Ⓑ why children like running and hopping games.
   - Ⓒ that running and hopping games have been played for many years.
   - Ⓓ why people play tag and hopscotch differently today.

2. List three running and hopping games.

_____

_____

_____

Games with Words

1. What are two kinds of word games?

    Ⓐ running games and clapping games

    Ⓑ color games and guessing games

    Ⓒ guessing games and clapping games

    Ⓓ clapping games and ball games

2. What do people need to play word games?

    _____

    _____

    _____

Connect Your Ideas

1. How are the things used in games long ago different from the things used in games today?

    _____

    _____

    _____

2. Would you rather play the games of long ago or the games of today? Why?

    _____

    _____

    _____

Transportation Then and Now

Before cars were invented, people rode in coaches that were pulled by horses.

Transportation in America

You may have come to school today on a bicycle, in a car, or on a bus. Bicycles, cars, and buses are[25] kinds of transportation. Transportation is the name for the ways people use to go from place to place.

When the United States was a new[50] country in 1776, there were not many kinds of transportation. People rode on horses or in coaches that were pulled by horses. There were also[75] boats, if people needed to go across water. It could take weeks or months to get from one place to another. No one traveled by[100] bicycle, train, car, or airplane. Bicycles, trains, cars, and airplanes had not been invented yet.[115]

Transportation Then and Now

Trains help people go from city to city.

Trains

Before there were trains, it took at least two months to get from the east to the west of the United States. Then train[25] tracks went from the east to the west of the United States. The trip on a train took only eight days.

Today, more people travel[50] across the country on airplanes than on trains. Yet trains are still very important. One train can pull many cars loaded with goods. Heavy loads[75] like cars and steel are often moved on trains. Trains are also used for transportation. With trains, people can get to work without using cars.[100] In some cities, trains travel underground. Trains also move people from city to city.[114]

Transportation Then and Now

About 100 years ago, bicycles began to look like bicycles today.

Bicycles

Today, children often ride bicycles for fun. When bicycles were first invented, they were only for grown-ups. The first bicycles had a big[25] wheel in front and a small wheel in back. The seat was high and was over the big wheel. It was easy to fall off[50] this bicycle.

About 120 years ago, bicycles were invented that look like the ones we use today. These bicycles had wheels of the same size.[75] The seat was over the back wheel. The new bicycles were safer. People rode them to work and to go on short trips. Bicycles are[100] still used for transportation. However, now bicycles are for everyone, not just for grown-ups.[115]

Transportation Then and Now

Henry Ford is riding in one of the cars he made.

Cars

The car was invented not long after the bicycle. The first cars looked a lot like bicycles. However, people didn't need to do the[25] work with their feet to make cars move. Cars used gas to move. Soon after, trucks, vans, and buses were invented, too.

The first cars[50] were made by hand and cost a lot of money. Then, a man named Henry Ford found a fast way to make cars. Soon, other[75] people began making cars the same way as Henry Ford. Cars became cheap enough for many people to own. Cars, trucks, vans, and buses are[100] different forms of transportation. They make travel easy for many people.[111]

Transportation Then and Now

Airplanes help people go from place to place.

Airplanes

Airplanes are the newest kind of transportation. From early times, people tried to fly through the sky like birds. About 100 years ago, someone[25] took the first ride on an airplane. This ride lasted for less than one minute. These first planes were very small, too. Only one or[50] two people could fly in them at one time.

Today, airplanes are very big and fast. Hundreds of people can travel in an airplane at[75] one time. With airplanes, people can get from one side of the United States to the other in less than one day. Travel is very[100] different today from the way it was 100 years ago.[110]

Write words that will help you remember what you learned.

Transportation in America

_____

_____

_____

Trains

_____

_____

_____

_____

Bicycles

_____

_____

_____

_____

Cars

_____

_____

_____

_____

Airplanes

_____

_____

_____

_____

Transportation in America

1. How did people travel in 1776?

    Ⓐ by trains, boats, and horses

    Ⓑ by cars, buses, and bicycles

    Ⓒ by horses, coaches pulled by horses, and boats

    Ⓓ by horses, boats, and bicycles

2. What is transportation?

_____

_____

_____

Trains

1. The main idea of "Trains" is _____

    Ⓐ how long it takes to travel across the country by train.

    Ⓑ where trains go today.

    Ⓒ how many people travel by train.

    Ⓓ how people use trains.

2. What are trains used for?

_____

_____

_____

Bicycles

1. How did the first bicycles look?

    Ⓐ They had two small wheels.

    Ⓑ They had a big wheel in front and a small wheel in back.

    Ⓒ They had two large wheels.

    Ⓓ They had a big wheel in front and two small wheels in back.

2. How have people used bicycles over the years?

    _____

    _____

    _____

Cars

1. "Cars" is MAINLY about _____

    Ⓐ how cars changed transportation.

    Ⓑ the way cars look today.

    Ⓒ Henry Ford.

    Ⓓ how much cars cost long ago.

2. Why are so many people able to buy cars today?

    _____

    _____

    _____

Airplanes

1. Another good name for "Airplanes" is ____

Ⓐ "Airplanes Then and Now."

Ⓑ "Fast Airplanes."

Ⓒ "Transportation Today."

Ⓓ "How Airplanes Work."

2. How has air travel changed from the first airplanes?

_____

_____

_____

Connect Your Ideas

1. How do people travel differently today from 100 years ago?

_____

_____

_____

2. What kind of transportation do you think people might use 100 years from now?

_____

_____

_____

Life in Colonial America

Ships like this one brought people from England to North America.

What Was Colonial America?

Over 400 years ago, a ship brought people from England to live in North America. After that, many more ships brought[25] people from England and many other places. The people lived in 13 places in North America that were called colonies.

The colonies were far from[50] England, but people in England ruled the colonies. In the year 1776, the people in the 13 colonies told England that they had made their[75] own country. They called this country the United States. When we talk about colonial America, we talk about the 13 colonies before 1776. Life in[100] colonial America was different from life in the United States today.[111]

Life in Colonial America

Corn was an important food in colonial America.

An Important New Food

When the first ships of colonists reached North America, the colonists had very little food left. The Native Americans shared food[25] with them. The Native Americans had food that was new to the colonists. Corn was the most important of the new foods. It was not[50] hard to grow corn in North America.

Corn had many uses. Corn on the cob was good to eat. Dried corn could be ground into[75] flour. The flour was used for baking. One kind of dried corn could be made into popcorn. Corn was used for animal food, too. In[100] winter, animals were fed the long stems of the corn plant.[111]

The colonists built houses with steep roofs so the snow could slide off the roofs.

Houses

As soon as they landed in North America, people had to build homes. Their first homes were made out of logs that they cut[25] into pieces. There were often big cracks between the logs. The cracks were filled with mud and grass. If the mud and grass fell out,[50] rain and snow came into the house.

Later, the colonists built houses that looked like their old homes in England. Many houses had flat roofs.[75] Soon, the colonists found that they needed to change their houses. It snowed more in parts of the 13 colonies than in England. People began[100] to build houses with steep roofs. Steep roofs let the snow slide off the roofs.[115]

Boys and girls went to Dame Schools.

School

In colonial America, children first went to Dame Schools. Dame Schools were in teachers' houses. Teachers used hornbooks to teach reading in Dame Schools.[25] A hornbook was a block of wood with a page of letters or words on it. It was called a hornbook because a thin sheet[50] of cow's horn was put over the letters and words. The sheet of cow's horn kept the letters and words clean. A clean hornbook could[75] be used for many years.

When girls could read, they stopped going to school. Boys went to another school where boys of all ages were[100] in one class. They had to sit still. They could not move around or talk.[115]

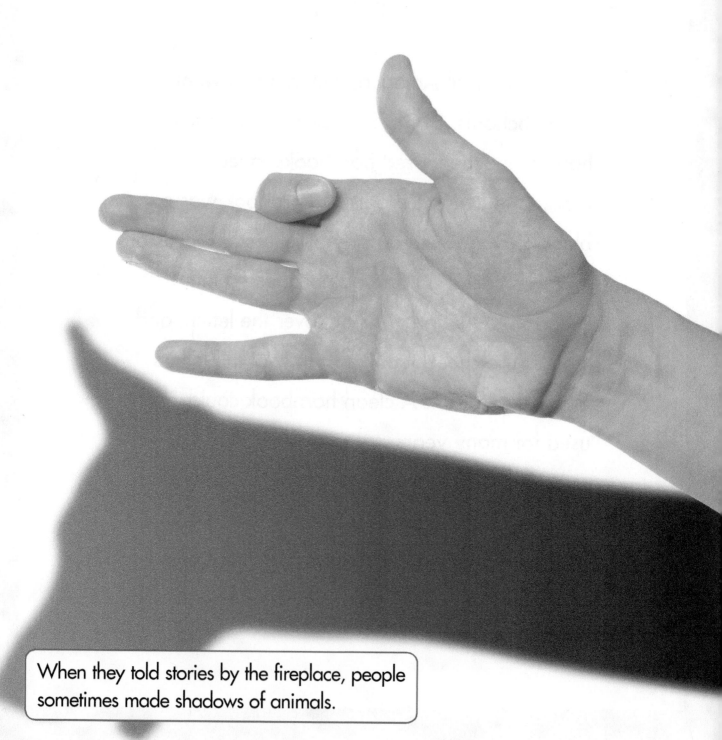

When they told stories by the fireplace, people sometimes made shadows of animals.

Shadow Stories

Even children worked hard in colonial America. Yet, there were times for fun, too. Children played tag. They skated on ice. During the[25] long, cold winters, children played games inside. While children played games close to the warm fireplace, someone told a story. Sometimes, storytellers would put their[50] hands in front of the fire. The firelight made a shadow on the wall. Storytellers would shape their hands to make the shadows look like[75] animals or people from the story.

You can tell shadow stories, too. Ask someone to point a flashlight at a wall. Hold your hands away[100] from the flashlight. Now make your hands into the shapes of different animals.[113]

Write words that will help you remember what you learned.

What Was Colonial America?

_____

_____

_____

An Important New Food

_____

_____

_____

Houses

_____

_____

_____

_____

School

_____

_____

_____

_____

Shadow Stories

_____

_____

_____

_____

What Was Colonial America?

1. How did people begin the North American colonies?

   Ⓐ People began to live in towns in England.

   Ⓑ People moved from England to North America.

   Ⓒ People moved from the United States to England.

   Ⓓ People moved from the United States to the colonies.

2. What was colonial America?

   _____

   _____

   _____

An Important New Food

1. Another good name for "An Important New Food" is _____

   Ⓐ "Sharing Food."

   Ⓑ "A New Food for the Colonists."

   Ⓒ "Food from England."

   Ⓓ "Native American Foods."

2. Name three ways the colonists used corn.

   _____

   _____

   _____

Review Life in Colonial America

Houses

1. What is the main idea of "Houses"?
   Ⓐ how colonists learned to build houses from mud
   Ⓑ how houses have changed over the years
   Ⓒ what houses in colonial America were like
   Ⓓ how to build a house in North America today

2. What three different kinds of houses did the colonists build?

_____

_____

_____

School

1. "School" is MAINLY about _____
   Ⓐ girls going to school in colonial America.
   Ⓑ how children went to school in colonial America.
   Ⓒ the books students read in colonial America.
   Ⓓ what teachers were like in colonial America.

2. What was school like in colonial America?

_____

_____

_____

Shadow Stories

1. What is a shadow story?

   Ⓐ a story about shadows

   Ⓑ a story about games that is told at night

   Ⓒ a story that is acted out

   Ⓓ a story told by making shadows on a wall

2. Name two ways children had fun in colonial America.

   _____

   _____

   _____

Connect Your Ideas

1. Name three ways that life changed for the colonists who came to live in North America.

   _____

   _____

   _____

2. What would your life have been like in colonial America?

   _____

   _____

   _____

Magnets

Magnets can hold papers on refrigerator doors.

What Do Magnets Do?

Many people have pictures on the door of their refrigerator. If you look closely, you will see that the pictures are[25] held in place by magnets. Most magnets are made of iron. They stick to other things with iron in them. Magnets stick to refrigerator doors[50] because refrigerator doors have iron in them.

The magnetic force holding the magnet to the door acts right through the picture. If you tried to[75] hang a picture on a wall using a magnet, the magnet and the picture would just fall to the floor. Why don't they stay up?[100] They don't stay up because most walls do not have iron in them.[113]

Magnets

Magnets can pick up paper clips because paper clips have iron in them.

Make Your Own Magnet

You can make your own magnet with a pin. Pins can be magnets because pins have iron in them. Pennies cannot[25] be magnets because pennies do not have iron in them.

To make a magnet, drag a pin along one end of a magnet. Drag the[50] pin only in one direction. Don't move it back and forth. Drag the pin in the same direction about 25 times. Your pin should now[75] act like a magnet. You will not be able to pick up heavy things with your new magnet, but you should be able to pick[100] up light things. See if your pin will pick up a paper clip.[113]

The poles of these magnets are pulling them together.

North and South

The ends of magnets are called "poles." One end of a magnet is its north pole. The other end is its south[25] pole. The poles of magnets, not the magnet's center, pull things to them. When there is more than one magnet, it matters what direction the[50] magnets are to each other.

If you put two magnets together, the magnets stick together or push each other away. When the north poles or[75] the south poles of two magnets face each other, the magnets push each other away. However, if you put the north pole of one magnet[100] against the south pole of another magnet, they will stick together.[111]

Magnets

The magnetic needle on a compass helps people find the right direction.

Finding the Right Direction

It can be fun to get magnets to stick to each other. However, magnets can help people, too. The Earth has[25] a lot of iron inside it. This iron and some other forces help Earth act like a really big magnet.

A magnetic needle will point[50] to the magnetic north pole of Earth. This is how a compass works. No matter which way a compass is turned, its needle points to[75] the magnetic north pole of Earth. With a compass, people can always tell which way is north. With a compass, people can go to new[100] places and not get lost. They can always find the right direction.[112]

Magnets

The black strips on bankcards are magnets.

Everyday Uses of Magnets

Magnets are used in many ways. Some ways are to hold pictures on refrigerators and to find directions with compasses. The[25] bankcards that people use to buy things in stores have magnets. The black strips on the back of bankcards are tiny magnets. These magnets store[50] information that tells the bank about the person.

Videotapes also use magnets. Like bankcards, videotapes have tiny magnets. The VCR uses them to make the[75] picture. The magnets that are in bankcards and videotapes are so tiny that you can't see them. However, these magnets act just like a magnet[100] you might make from a pin or the magnets on a refrigerator.[112]

Review Magnets

Write words that will help you remember what you learned.

What Do Magnets Do?

_____

_____

_____

_____

Make Your Own Magnet

_____

_____

_____

_____

North and South

_____

_____

_____

_____

Finding the Right Direction

_____

_____

_____

_____

Everyday Uses of Magnets

_____

_____

_____

_____

What Do Magnets Do?

1. "What Do Magnets Do?" is MAINLY about _____
   Ⓐ how magnets work.
   Ⓑ different kinds of magnets.
   Ⓒ the many uses of magnets.
   Ⓓ magnets on refrigerator doors.

2. What do magnets do?

_____

_____

_____

Make Your Own Magnet

1. What is the main idea of "Make Your Own Magnet"?
   Ⓐ how pins are magnets
   Ⓑ how to use a magnet
   Ⓒ how to make a magnet
   Ⓓ why people make magnets

2. How can you make a pin into a magnet?

_____

_____

_____

Review Magnets

North and South

1. What are poles on magnets?
   Ⓐ the parts of magnets that are hot
   Ⓑ the parts of magnets that go the same way
   Ⓒ the ends of magnets
   Ⓓ the centers of magnets

2. How can you make two magnets stick together?

_____

_____

_____

Finding the Right Direction

1. How can magnets help people?
   Ⓐ Magnets can help people find Earth.
   Ⓑ Magnets are giant compasses.
   Ⓒ Magnets can keep people from getting lost.
   Ⓓ Magnetic needles have iron inside them.

2. What does a compass do?

_____

_____

_____

Everyday Uses of Magnets

1. Another good name for "Everyday Uses of Magnets" is _____

Ⓐ "Magnets in Your Home."

Ⓑ "Magnets People Wear."

Ⓒ "Magnets in School."

Ⓓ "The Many Uses of Magnets."

2. What are three ways we use magnets?

_____

_____

_____

Connect Your Ideas

1. Name three things that a magnet can stick to.

_____

_____

_____

2. What do you think is the most important way to use magnets? Why?

_____

_____

_____

You can move a wagon by pushing it or pulling it.

Push and Pull

You and your friends are playing with a wagon. One friend gets into the wagon and asks you to move it. How[25] can you move the wagon? You can push it or pull it. When you push or pull the wagon, you use force. By using force,[50] you can move the wagon from place to place.

What if your friend asks you to make the wagon move faster? You can use more[75] force. If your friend is small, it will not take much force to go faster. However, if your friend is big, it will take a[100] lot more force to go faster. Force makes things move.[110]

Forces Around Us

You use force when you move a toy car.

Work and Play

You are playing with a toy car. Whenever you move the toy car, we say that you are doing work. Work happens[25] when a force is used to move something.

If you use a lot of force to move something, you are doing a lot of work.[50] It is more work to move a box of toy cars than to move one toy car. Even when you play, you may be doing[75] work.

If you push a real car but it does not move, you are not doing work. Why? The force you use is too small[100] to move the car. A force has to move something to do work.[113]

Forces Around Us

You are doing work when you are riding your bicycle.

Energy and Work

When you take out the trash, you do work. When you lift a heavy book, you do work. When you and your[25] friends ride your bikes, you all do work. Work happens when you use force to make something move. Yet, how does the force do the[50] work? The force does the work by using energy.

You must have energy to do work. If you do a lot of work, you use[75] a lot of energy. If you do just a little work, you don't use very much energy. You get energy from food. Cars get energy[100] from gas. If there is energy, work can be done.[110]

Forces Around Us

Gravity keeps you from jumping up too high.

Up and Down

Why can't you jump ten feet in the air? Gravity holds you down. Gravity is the force that pulls you back to [25] Earth.

Why can you toss a ball ten feet in the air? It does not take much force to toss a ball because a ball [50] does not have much mass. It takes less force to move things with less mass.

You have more mass than a ball. So it would [75] take more force for you to jump ten feet in the air than to toss a ball ten feet in the air. Moving an object [100] with a lot of mass against the force of gravity takes a lot of energy. [115]

Forces Around Us

Friction makes it hard to drag a chair over a rug.

Smooth and Rough

If you have ever tried to move an object like a heavy chair, you know about friction. A heavy chair is hard[25] to drag over something rough like a rug. The chair does not move easily because it rubs against the rug. The force that makes it[50] hard to drag one thing over another is called friction.

A heavy chair is easy to move over a slick floor. That is because there[75] is less friction between objects and smooth surfaces, such as a slick floor. There is more friction between objects and rough surfaces, such as a[100] rug. If there is less friction, it is easier to move something.[112]

Write words that will help you remember what you learned.

Push and Pull

_____

_____

_____

_____

Work and Play

_____

_____

_____

_____

Energy and Work

_____

_____

_____

_____

Up and Down

_____

_____

_____

_____

Smooth and Rough

_____

_____

_____

_____

Push and Pull

1. What can happen when you use force?

   Ⓐ You can make a wagon.

   Ⓑ You can make something move.

   Ⓒ You can play a game with your friends.

   Ⓓ You can go from place to place.

2. Retell two facts you learned in "Push and Pull."

_____

_____

_____

Work and Play

1. Another good name for "Work and Play" is _____

   Ⓐ "Force and Work."

   Ⓑ "Playing with Cars."

   Ⓒ "How to Work."

   Ⓓ "Moving Things."

2. When does work happen?

_____

_____

_____

Review Forces Around Us

Energy and Work

1. Why do you need energy?

   Ⓐ to sit still

   Ⓑ to get force

   Ⓒ to make more energy

   Ⓓ to do work

2. How do people and cars get energy?

   _____

   _____

   _____

Up and Down

1. What is "Up and Down" MAINLY about?

   Ⓐ what mass is

   Ⓑ what different forces are

   Ⓒ how gravity works

   Ⓓ why people can jump ten feet in the air

2. What is gravity?

   _____

   _____

   _____

Smooth and Rough

1. Friction is the force that _____

   Ⓐ makes it hard to drag one thing over another.

   Ⓑ keeps you from jumping high in the air.

   Ⓒ tells you when something is smooth or rough.

   Ⓓ gives you energy to move things.

2. Why is it easier to move something over a smooth surface than over a rough surface?

   _____

   _____

   _____

Connect Your Ideas

1. Tell about two forces you learned about.

   _____

   _____

   _____

2. Name two ways you use energy every day.

   _____

   _____

   _____

Thinking Like a Scientist

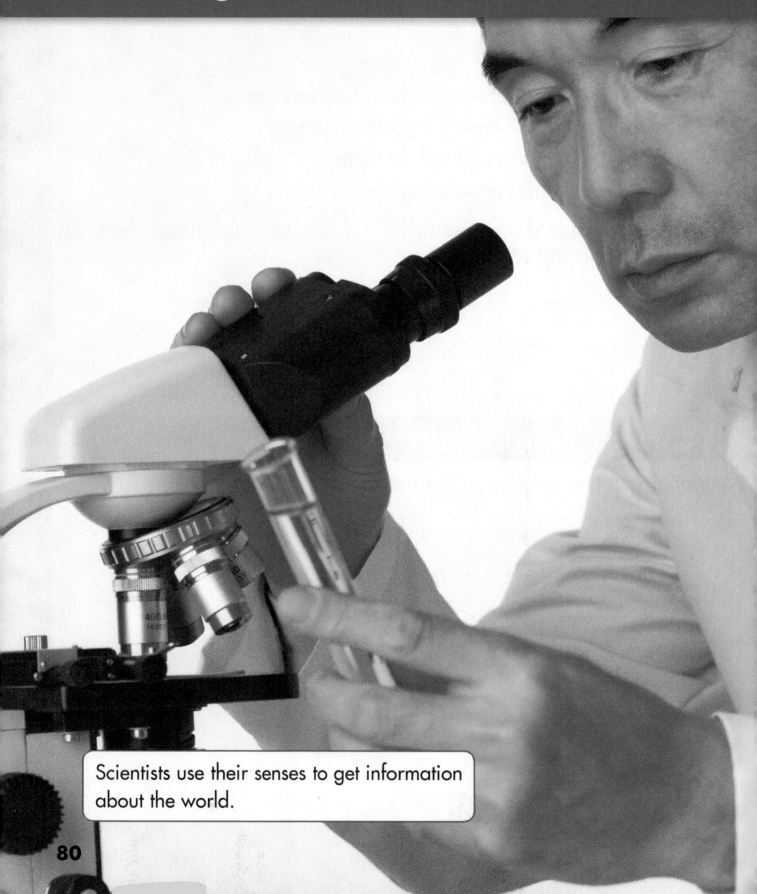

Scientists use their senses to get information about the world.

Asking Questions

The word *science* means "knowledge."
Scientists are people who study the world to get
knowledge or information. Scientists ask how
things work. They[25] use their senses to get
knowledge. They think about what they learn.
First, scientists ask questions. Then, they look for
information to answer questions.

Where[50] do the colors of a rainbow come
from? There are many colors in a rainbow: red,
orange, yellow, green, blue, and purple. Light
doesn't look[75] like it has color. Yet, rainbows have
the colors red, orange, yellow, green, blue, and
purple. What happens to the colors when the
rainbow goes[100] away? When you ask questions
like these, you are thinking like a scientist.[113]

Thinking Like a Scientist

Your senses can help you learn about the world around you.

Using Your Senses

To get new knowledge, you use parts of your body called your senses. Your senses help you see, hear, touch, taste, and [25] smell. You see with your eyes. Your ears let you hear sounds. You touch things with your skin, usually your hands. You taste with your [50] mouth. You use your nose to find out how things smell.

Scientists use their senses to get new information, too. However, scientists are careful in [75] how they use their senses. They never taste unknown things. Scientists are careful about what they touch. Scientists also take care of their eyes, ears, [100] and noses when they work with things that can hurt them. [111]

Thinking Like a Scientist

These young scientists take notes as they study the world.

Taking Notes

Scientists study the world to get information. Then, scientists take notes about what they learn. They take notes with pictures and numbers, not[25] just words. Scientists who study the colors in sunlight might write about the colors they see. They also might write about the colors they don't[50] see.

Scientists use their notes to see what is the same and what is different about things. Scientists have found that the colors in a[75] rainbow can be seen through a three-sided piece of glass called a prism. When sunlight passes through a prism, the sunlight comes out as[100] bands of color. Scientists use their notes about color to learn more about sunlight.[114]

Thinking Like a Scientist

Tests help scientists see if their guesses are right.

Doing Tests

Scientists use their notes to make guesses about how things work. Scientists do tests to see if their guesses are right. Scientists now[25] know that the colors of the rainbow are in sunlight all the time. However, something like a prism is needed to bring the colors out.[50] You can do tests like a scientist, too. Just use your senses and take notes about what you learn.

You can test the colors in[75] sunlight. Poke a small hole in a piece of tinfoil. Place the tinfoil over the lens of a flashlight. Now take a CD into a[100] dark room. Shine the flashlight onto the CD. What do you see?[112]

Eugenie Clark studies sharks by asking questions about them.

A Shark Scientist

Eugenie Clark is a scientist who studies sharks. Eugenie began asking questions like a scientist when she was nine years old. That's [25] when she got a fish tank as a gift. She made notes and pictures about the fish.

Many people think that danger comes from big [50] sharks. However, Eugenie Clark thinks that sharks may face more danger from people than people do from sharks. She found that the biggest shark of [75] all, the whale shark, eats only small sea animals and plants. Eugenie Clark learned about sharks by using her senses, taking notes, and doing tests [100] on sharks. That information will help people understand how to safely live with sharks. [114]

Write words that will help you remember what you learned.

Asking Questions

_____

_____

_____

_____

Using Your Senses

_____

_____

_____

_____

Taking Notes

_____

_____

_____

_____

Doing Tests

_____

_____

_____

_____

A Shark Scientist

_____

_____

_____

_____

Asking Questions

1. A scientist is someone who _____

    Ⓐ uses force to do work.

    Ⓑ writes stories about the world.

    Ⓒ studies the world to get knowledge.

    Ⓓ studies things that happened long ago.

2. How can you think like a scientist?

_____

_____

_____

Using Your Senses

1. What are your senses?

    Ⓐ the way you use your nose to learn how things smell

    Ⓑ touching, seeing, hearing, thinking, and jumping

    Ⓒ how you learn about other people

    Ⓓ seeing, hearing, touching, tasting, and smelling

2. How are scientists careful with their senses?

_____

_____

_____

Review Thinking Like a Scientist

Taking Notes

1. "Taking Notes" is MAINLY about _____

Ⓐ how scientists take and use notes.

Ⓑ how scientists draw pictures.

Ⓒ where scientists get ideas.

Ⓓ how scientists know what to study.

2. What do scientists do with their notes?

_____

_____

_____

Doing Tests

1. Another good name for "Doing Tests" is _____

Ⓐ "Scientists Use Their Senses."

Ⓑ "Guesses and Tests."

Ⓒ "The Colors of the Rainbow."

Ⓓ "Taking Good Notes."

2. Why do scientists do tests?

_____

_____

_____

A Shark Scientist

1. The main idea of "A Shark Scientist" is _____

  Ⓐ Eugenie Clark's work as a shark scientist.

  Ⓑ how shark scientists work.

  Ⓒ the kinds of sharks Eugenie Clark studies.

  Ⓓ why sharks face danger from people.

2. What did Eugenie Clark learn about sharks?

_____

_____

_____

Connect Your Ideas

1. How can you think like a scientist every day?

_____

_____

_____

2. What would you like to study if you were a scientist?

_____

_____

_____

Reading Log • Level B • Book 3

	I Read This	New Words I Learned	New Facts I Learned	What Else I Want to Learn About This Subject
Children's Games				
Games of Then and Now				
Games with Balls				
Games with Toys				
Games of Running and Hopping				
Games with Words				
Transportation Then and Now				
Transportation in America				
Trains				
Bicycles				
Cars				
Airplanes				
Life in Colonial America				
What Was Colonial America?				
An Important New Food				
Houses				
School				
Shadow Stories				

	I Read This	New Words I Learned	New Facts I Learned	What Else I Want to Learn About This Subject
Magnets				
What Do Magnets Do?				
Make Your Own Magnet				
North and South				
Finding the Right Direction				
Everyday Uses of Magnets				
Forces Around Us				
Push and Pull				
Work and Play				
Energy and Work				
Up and Down				
Smooth and Rough				
Thinking Like a Scientist				
Asking Questions				
Using Your Senses				
Taking Notes				
Doing Tests				
A Shark Scientist				

Self-Check Graph

Column headers (reading rate categories):
- Games of Then and Now
- Games with Balls
- Games with Toys
- Games of Running and Hopping
- Games with Words
- Transportation in America
- Trains
- Bicycles
- Cars
- Airplanes
- What Was Colonial America?
- An Important New Food
- Houses
- School
- Shadow Stories
- What Do Magnets Do?
- Make Your Own Magnet
- North and South
- Finding the Right Direction
- Everyday Uses of Magnets
- Push and Pull
- Work and Play
- Energy and Work
- Up and Down
- Smooth and Rough
- Asking Questions
- Using Your Senses
- Taking Notes
- Doing Tests
- A Shark Scientist

Vertical axis values (top to bottom): 130, 128, 126, 124, 122, 120, 118, 116, 114, 112, 110, 108, 106, 104, 102, 100, 98, 96, 94, 92, 90, 88, 86, 84, 82, 80, 78, 76, 74, 72, 70, 68, 66, 64, 62, 60, 58, 56, 54, 52, 50

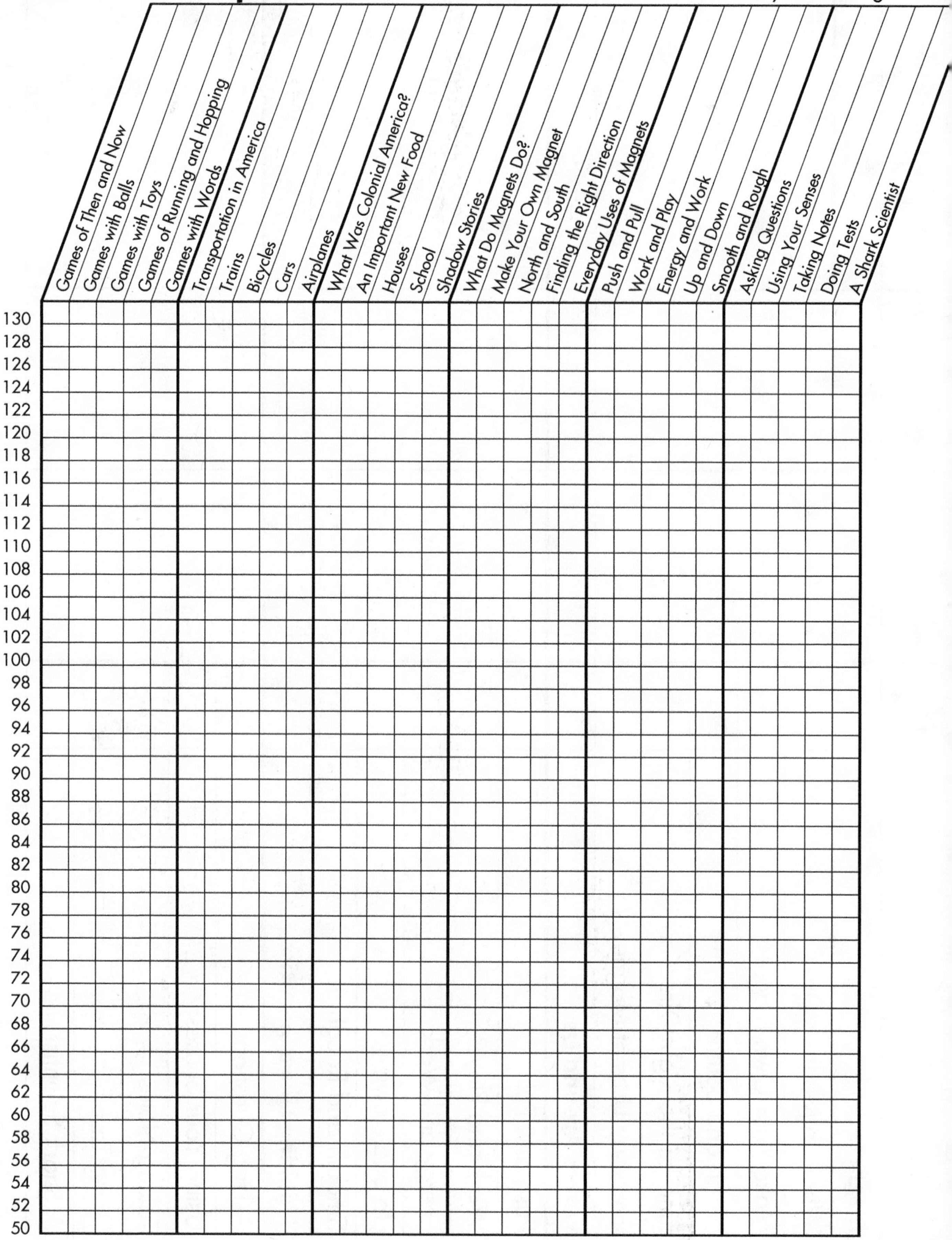